D0427577

THE BEST LITTLE
MARINADES
COOKBOOK

by Karen Adler

CELESTIAL ARTS
Berkeley

Special thanks to
Mary Ann Duckers, Judith Fertig, Dennis Hayes, Dane Herbel,
Karen Putman, Veronica Randall, Lou Jane Temple,
and my associates at Celestial Arts
for their contributions to this book.

Copyright © 2000 by Karen Adler.

Library of Congress Catalog Card Number: 00-131236
Library of Congress Cataloging-in-Publication Data is on file with
the publisher.

ISBN: 978-0-89087-964-1

Printed in Malaysia.

Cover design: Catherine Jacobes
Cover art: Paul Keppel
Interior illustrations: Barry's Clip Art, Basting brush by Brad Greene
Text design: Greene Design

Other cookbooks in this series:
Best Little Barbecue Cookbook
Best Little BBQ Sauces Cookbook
Best Little Grilling Cookbook

16 15 14 13 12 11 10 9 8

First Edition

INTRODUCTION

In times past it was common for foods to be cooked and served buried in spices, brined in salt, or preserved with vinegars. All of these techniques enhanced the flavor and often added shelf life, too—an important feature in the days before refrigeration. Today's global cuisine has evolved to include a variety of cooking techniques and exotic ingredients. But our hectic lifestyles make it hard to cook with flavor and style and an eye toward healthful living.

Marinades, rubs, and pastes are those delightful blends of oils, vinegars, spices, seasonings, and herbs that have come into their own as a part of this enlightened culinary revolution. Their combination of versatility, speed, and simplicity appeals to today's creative cook and has become synonymous with outdoor grilling. Imagine never tasting a fresh grilled salmon flavored with ginger, garlic, and sesame oil. What would a barbecued rib dinner be without the zestiness of a peppery rub that's applied before cooking? And a leg of lamb just wouldn't be the same without a garlicky pesto paste. These exciting seasonings have recently been catapulted into the spotlight, so grab a whisk and let's get cooking!

The Basics

Marinades, rubs, and pastes are flavorful combinations applied to meats and vegetables prior to cooking. They are used to season food for pan sautéing, oven broiling, baking, grilling, and smoking.

A liquid marinade is fundamentally a mixture of an acidlike vinegar or citrus combined with a cooking oil. Pungent aromatics are added for more complexity and include herbs, seasonings, onions, garlic, and condiments like soy sauce, mustard, and horse-radish.

A rub is traditionally a mixture of dry seasonings that can be kept for several months stored away from light in a tightly covered glass jar. When fresh ingredients like herbs from the garden or grated cheeses are combined, they may still be used as a rub, but will not have the extended shelf life of the dry rub counterpart. The basic ingredients for a rub are salt, black pepper, and paprika. Other essential items include chili powder, celery seed, crushed red pepper or ground red pepper, cinnamon, and cumin. Any of the following herbs are enhancements to the rub mix: basil, dill, marjoram, oregano, parsley, rosemary, sage, tarragon, and thyme.

Pastes are in between a rub and a marinade. Add a small amount of liquid to a rub and it becomes a thick paste. The fastest way to make a paste is to lightly coat the meat with oil, then sprinkle on the rub. Also fresh ingredients like herbs, citrus zest, garlic, and onions combined in a food processor with a little bit of oil make a paste. Pesto is an excellent example of a paste.

Marinades, rubs, and pastes are a delicious flavoring agent that add a zesty tang of flavor to the food we cook. Marinades also help to keep foods from drying out. They are not quite a tenderizer, but they do help add moisture to tough cuts of meats when marinated for several hours or overnight in the refrigerator.

Tips for making marinades, rubs, and pastes. Mix it up and rub it in. It's that easy. A coffee grinder or a mini food processor works nicely for blending and grinding ingredients for dry rubs. A non-reactive stainless steel or glass bowl and a whisk make easy work of assembling a marinade or paste. Or use a glass jar that has a tight-fitting lid to combine the ingredients. Screw on the lid and they are ready for storage, plus you'll minimize the cleanup.

Do's and don'ts. Marinades usually have an acidic element, so use only nonreactive materials like glass, stainless steel, and plastic for mixing and marinating. One of the easiest ways to marinate is to use a large sealable plastic bag. Place the items to be marinated in first, then pour in the marinade, seal the bag, and put it in the refrigerator.

Do not reuse marinades. Once a marinade has come into contact with meat, it is exposed to bacteria. Some recipes will advise boiling the exposed marinade for several minutes to use as a dipping sauce, but do not save the marinade after that. Likewise, when applying a rub, it is best to sprinkle the rub onto your meat so the uncontaminated rub in the jar may be stored for later use.

Find a few combinations of rubs that suit you best. Make them in quantities to last for 2 or 3 months. Add a dash of rub to your stews, soups, whatever you're cooking that needs a little boost. Store these mixtures in a glass jar with a tight-fitting lid. Make a double batch of your best rub and share it with a favorite friend.

A word of warning: over-marinating can cause mushiness. Marinate tender cuts of meat like fish and chicken breasts for only 30 to 60 minutes. Beef steaks and pork chops may be marinated for 30 minutes to several hours. Tough cuts like brisket and roasts may be marinated overnight. Always marinate in the refrigerator.

MARINADES

The Perfect Pantry

Stocking the pantry is a wonderful way to save time. Many of the dry or packaged ingredients needed for marinades, rubs, and pastes have a shelf life of several months or longer. Your preferences will dictate the items that you'll keep on hand. As you experiment with more exotic flavors, your pantry staples will grow. Here's a list of essentials for a basic marinade pantry.

Basic seasonings: assorted pepper and pepper blends such as lemon pepper or seasoned pepper; preferred salts are sea or kosher salt; flavored salts include garlic, onion, and celery; garlic and onion powders. Chilies to stock include chili powder, paprika, red pepper, and red pepper flakes. Keep brown and white sugar and honey on hand as sweeteners.

Dried herbs: basil, oregano, parsley, rosemary, tarragon, sage, thyme, mint, bay leaves, and chives. Spices include dry mustard, ground ginger, cinnamon, cloves, coriander, and cumin.

Basic vinegars and oils: distilled white vinegar, cider vinegar, vegetable, olive, and/or peanut oil. Get fancy with wine, rice, balsamic, and assorted herb vinegars, and upscale your oil selections with sesame, walnut, and garlic oil or make your own (pages 17 to 19).

Condiments: mustards, soy sauce, Worcestershire, hot sauces, liquors, beers, liqueurs, fruit juices, store-bought marinades, and grill seasonings.

Marinades

SATAY MARINADE

This is an excellent Asian-style marinade for beef, pork, poultry, seafood—from whole tenderloins or birds to kabobs.

1/2 cup soy sauce

1/2 cup rice wine vinegar

1/2 cup chunky peanut butter

1/3 cup chopped cilantro

2 tablespoons dark honey

1 tablespoon toasted sesame oil or tahini

1 tablespoon freshly grated ginger

Zest and juice of 1 lime

2 cloves garlic, minced

1/2 teaspoon red pepper flakes

Combine all ingredients and mix well. Pour mixture over meat or vegetables and marinate for 30 to 60 minutes in the refrigerator.

Makes 1 cup

Patio Steak Marinade

Patio steaks or charcoal steaks are tasty, inexpensive cuts of meat from the beef shoulder. They need to marinate for several hours or overnight to make them succulent and juicy.

2 cloves garlic, minced

2 teaspoons dried basil

2 teaspoons dried oregano

1 teaspoon Szechuan-style black pepper

1/3 cup olive oil

1/4 cup cider vinegar

1 large red onion, sliced

Combine garlic, basil, oregano, and pepper, then add oil and vinegar. (Fresh basil or oregano may be substituted for the dry version by doubling the amount.) Place meat of choice, sliced red onion, and marinade in a large sealable plastic bag and refrigerate.

Makes about 3/4 cup

Tamarind Marinade

Shellfish are spectacular marinated in this mixture. It also works well with poultry, pork, and other seafood, too.

¹/₄ cup vegetable oil

¹/₄ cup hoisin sauce

¹/₄ cup tamarind juice

¹/₄ cup brown sugar

¹/₄ cup chopped chives

1 tablespoon paprika

 Combine all of the ingredients in a glass jar. Store in the refrigerator for up to 1 week.

Makes about 1¹/₄ cups

Fresh Sliced Papaya with Soy

Papaya contains papain, a digestive enzyme used in meat tenderizers. Using the whole fruit—flesh, skin, and seeds—is a flavorful way to tenderize tough cuts of meat like flank, arm, tip, etc. Marinate tough cuts of meat overnight and tender meats like chicken breasts for only 2 or 3 hours.

1 papaya, sliced thin

2 tablespoons soy sauce

2 tablespoons sugar

Kosher salt and freshly ground pepper to taste

 Layer the bottom of a glass casserole with half of the papaya (including the seeds). Place the meat to be marinated on top of the papaya. Evenly distribute the soy sauce, sugar, salt, and pepper over the meat. Layer the remaining slices of papaya on top of the seasoned meat. Place a smaller casserole on top of the mixture to press the layers together and refrigerate.

Makes enough to marinate a flank steak or 6 to 8 chicken breasts

Fresh Crushed Pineapple Marinade

Marinate shrimp in this fragrant mixture, then grill.
Serve with jasmine rice and fresh grilled pineapple
slices for a taste of the exotic.

1 cup fresh crushed pineapple

1 cup coconut milk

3 tablespoons fish sauce (nam pla)

2 tablespoons red curry paste

2 tablespoons sugar

 Combine all of the ingredients and either use immediately or store in the refrigerator for up to 1 week.

Makes 2 1/2 cups

Pacific Islands Marinade

This is an easy way to get a taste of the islands in less than a minute. It enhances grilled ham, pork, poultry, and seafood.

½ cup teriyaki sauce

½ cup pineapple juice

1 teaspoon grated fresh ginger

Combine all of the ingredients in a glass jar. Mix well and store in the refrigerator.

Makes 1 cup

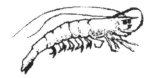

Fresh Mint Oil

Instead of mint jelly with lamb, try this oil, which acts as a flavoring and also helps to keep the lamb steaks or tenderloin from sticking to the grill.

1 cup fresh mint leaves, loosely packed

1 cup olive oil

Salt and freshly ground pepper to taste

Combine all of the ingredients in a blender or food processor. Process on high until mixture is puréed. Set aside to let the flavors infuse for several hours. Strain through a cheesecloth 2 or 3 times to remove the mint particles. Store in a cool dark cabinet. (If using right away, the mint does not need to be strained.)

Makes about 1 1/4 cups

Garlic-Pepper Oil

This all-purpose marinade is great on absolutely anything.

1/2 cup olive oil

2 tablespoons granulated garlic

2 tablespoons freshly cracked peppercorns

 Combine all of the ingredients in a glass jar. Mix well and store in the refrigerator.

Makes 3/4 cup

MARINADES

Herb-Infused Oil

Flavored oils are a snap to make. Use them in interesting vinaigrettes or give them as gourmet gifts.

1/2 cup fresh herbs, loosely packed (use "woody" herbs such as rosemary, thyme, sage, bay, oregano, etc.)

1 clove garlic, peeled

1 cup best-quality olive oil

Set aside the best leaves or sprigs to display in the bottle. Put the rest of the herbs and garlic in a saucepan with the oil. Heat gently for 20 minutes. Do not allow herbs to brown. Let oil cool, then strain. Save garlic clove. Put flavored oil, garlic clove, and best leaves or sprigs in a glass bottle. Cork and seal. As you use the oil, remove herbs if they aren't completely immersed. (Herbs will become moldy in bottle if not completely covered with oil.)

Makes 1 cup

Middle Eastern Apricot-Yogurt Marinade

This delicious combination of sweet and tangy flavors marries well with lamb, pork, and poultry.

1/2 cup minced onion

2 cloves garlic, minced

1 1/2 tablespoons chopped fresh parsley

3 teaspoons chopped dried apricots

1/2 teaspoon ground cinnamon

1/4 teaspoon ground ginger

1/2 cup plain yogurt

Salt and pepper to taste

Combine all of the ingredients in a glass jar. Mix well and store in the refrigerator. (May be blended in a food processor.)

Makes about 1 cup

Rocky Mountain Wild Game Marinade

This is an especially flavorful marinade for dark meat like elk, venison, and duck.

1 cup oil

1 cup white wine vinegar

10 allspice berries, crushed

10 cloves garlic, minced

1 tablespoon black pepper

1 teaspoon dried thyme leaves

1 teaspoon cayenne pepper

1 teaspoon dried basil

Combine all of the ingredients in a glass jar. Mix well and store in the refrigerator. Keeps refrigerated for up to 2 weeks.

Variation: instead of dried thyme, try 2 teaspoons fresh thyme, basil, oregano, or chives.

Makes 2 cups

Upland Game Bird Marinade

Dane Herbel grills quail with this marinade recipe that is good for all poultry. Marinate quail, pheasant, or chicken in a sealable plastic bag for 1 to 2 hours in the refrigerator, then grill or smoke.

1/2 cup soy sauce

1/4 cup olive oil

2 tablespoons Marsala

2 cloves garlic, minced

 Combine all of the ingredients in a glass jar. Mix well and store in the refrigerator.

Makes about 1 cup

Provençal White Wine Marinade

This is a lovely light marinade that is excellent for grilling or smoking poultry or seafood over soaked grape vines.

2/3 cup dry white wine (Chablis, Chardonnay, or Bordeaux)

1/3 cup olive oil

2 shallots, minced

1 tablespoon chopped fresh tarragon

1 tablespoon herbes de Provence (page 83)

1/2 teaspoon white pepper

1/2 teaspoon sea salt

Combine all of the ingredients in a glass jar. Mix well and store in the refrigerator.

Makes about 1 1/4 cups

French Herb Cream

Try cooking some new potatoes or sweet onions on the smoker or grill. When they are not quite done, place them in a casserole, pour the herb cream over them, and finish baking in the oven at 325 degrees F for 1 hour.

1/2 cup whipping cream

3 or 4 sprigs of herb of your choice (tarragon, rosemary, lavender, or parsley)

2 tablespoons snipped chives

Combine cream and herbs and use immediately as a marinade for poultry, potatoes, or onions that are to be grilled.

Does not keep well.

Makes 1/2 cup

Mustard-Tarragon Marinade

Dijon mustard and tarragon are a classic French combination. Use this mixture for seafood and poultry. It's also delicious as a dipping sauce for artichokes.

1/2 cup Dijon mustard

3 tablespoons olive oil

3 tablespoon lemon juice

8 to 10 sprigs fresh tarragon

 Combine all of the ingredients in a glass jar. Mix well and store in the refrigerator.

Makes about 3/4 cup

Tandoori Marinade

The flavors of India work beautifully with poultry, tuna steaks, skewered shrimp, and grilled scallops.

1 (2-inch-long) piece fresh ginger

1 cup yogurt

4 or 5 cloves garlic, minced

2 teaspoons ground cumin

2 teaspoons ground coriander

1 teaspoon cayenne pepper

1 teaspoon salt

4 tablespoons vegetable oil

 Peel ginger and grate or process to a paste. Combine with remaining ingredients in a glass bowl and use immediately.

Makes 1 1/2 cups

THAI VINAIGRETTE

A perfect marinade for grilled boneless meat. Use to marinate seafood, pork, or poultry. Serve over a bed of mixed greens for a complete meal. Reserve a portion of unused vinaigrette to drizzle over the finished composed salad.

1 cup peanut oil

1/4 cup fresh lime juice

1/4 cup rice vinegar

1 tablespoon fish sauce (nam pla)

1 tablespoon minced cilantro

1 tablespoon minced mint

1 serrano chile pepper, minced (may substitute jalapeño)

2 cloves garlic, minced

2 teaspoons sugar

1 teaspoon minced ginger

Combine all of the ingredients and whisk to blend thoroughly. Store for 2 to 3 days in the refrigerator.

Makes about 1 3/4 cups

Szechuan-Style Marinade

This spicy Chinese marinade is perfect for shellfish. Combine shrimp, scallops, green onion, and red bell pepper with this mixture for an excellent wok-grilled meal.

1/2 cup bottled Szechuan sauce

1/4 cup soy sauce

1/4 cup rice vinegar

1/4 cup dry sherry

1 tablespoon minced fresh ginger

Combine all of the ingredients in a glass jar. Shake to blend. Store in the refrigerator for up to 2 weeks.

Makes 1 1/4 cups

Asian Seafood Marinade

Marinate fish and seafood for no more than 30 minutes. Perfect for a quick meal that tastes like you cooked all day. Over-marinating causes the fish to get mushy.

1/4 cup hoisin sauce

2 tablespoons soy sauce

2 tablespoons rice vinegar

Combine all of the ingredients in a glass jar. Mix well and store in the refrigerator.

Makes about 1/2 cup

Grand Marnier Marinade

Poultry and seafood, especially shellfish, will wow any palate after some quality time in this simple but sophisticated marinade.

Juice and zest of 1 lemon

Juice and zest of 1 lime

3 tablespoons Grand Marnier

 Combine all of the ingredients in a glass jar. Mix well and store in the refrigerator.

Makes about 1/2 cup

Shenandoah Valley Vinegar Marinade

Originally created for North Carolina–style turkey, this marinade is also excellent for pork or poultry.

1/2 cup vinegar

1/3 cup peanut oil

1/2 tablespoon poultry seasoning

1/2 tablespoon black pepper

2 teaspoons salt

1 teaspoon garlic powder

1 teaspoon hot sauce

1 teaspoon lemon juice

Salt and pepper to taste

Combine all of the ingredients in a glass jar. Mix well and store in the refrigerator.

Makes 1 cup

Coca-Cola™ Marinade for Flank Steak

Chef Karen Putman has won hundreds of barbecue ribbons and trophies. She marinates flank steak with this recipe, so try it with the cut of your choice.

1 quart Coca-Cola™

2 cups oil

2 cups vinegar

6 cloves garlic

Salt and pepper to taste

Combine all of the ingredients in a glass jar. Mix well and store in the refrigerator.

Makes 2 quarts

Balsamic Marinade

An excellent marinade for turkey and other poultry or pork. Marinate overnight for best results.

1 cup balsamic vinegar

$1/4$ cup water

3 tablespoons paprika

2 tablespoons sea salt

2 tablespoons lemon pepper

$1/4$ teaspoon marjoram

Combine all of the ingredients in a glass jar. Mix well and store in the refrigerator.

Makes about 1$1/2$ cups

CABERNET-BALSAMIC STEAK MARINADE

Full-bodied Cabernet Sauvignon and rich Italian balsamic vinegar are perfect for marinating beef steaks and wild game.

1 red onion, sliced thinly into rings

1/2 cup Cabernet red wine

1/3 cup olive oil

1/4 cup balsamic vinegar

1 or 2 cloves garlic, crushed

8 to 10 fresh basil leaves, stripped from the stalks

Combine all of the ingredients and use immediately.

Makes about 1 cup

MEDITERRANEAN MARINADE

Think of the sunny beaches of the Spanish, French, and Italian Rivieras, then marinate and cook the seafood of your choice in this fragrant concoction.

6 green onions, chopped

3 tablespoons fresh lemon juice

1 cup extra virgin olive oil

2 teaspoons finely chopped fresh rosemary

Sea salt and freshly ground pepper to taste

Combine all of the ingredients in a glass jar. Mix well and store in the refrigerator.

Makes about 1 1/2 cups

Venezuelan Spice Marinade

This marinade is traditionally poured over a beef roast and is known as pabellon criollo.

2 cups crushed tomatoes

1 cup spicy tomato barbecue sauce

1/4 cup chopped fresh cilantro

1/4 cup chopped onion

1 red bell pepper, seeded and diced

3 cloves garlic, minced

2 teaspoons curry powder

Salt and pepper to taste

Combine all of the ingredients in a glass bowl and mix well. Use immediately to marinate the meat of your choice.

Makes 3 1/2 cups

Brew-Pub Marinade

Experiment with a pale ale, amber, lager, stout,
or beer of your choice.

Zest of 1 lemon

3 tablespoons sugar

1 tablespoon salt

1 teaspoon ground cloves

1 bottle of microbrewed beer

1/2 cup oil

1/4 cup minced onion

Dash of Tabasco sauce

In a large glass bowl, mix dry ingredients together and add enough beer to make a smooth paste. Whisk in oil. Add remaining beer, onion, and Tabasco to taste. Pour into a large glass jar with a tight-fitting lid. Leave at room temperature overnight and then refrigerate. Shake gently before using.

Makes 1 pint

Lemon-Herb Vinaigrette

This is a lovely marinade for vegetables and meats, or a great dressing for salad greens or tender young green beans.

2/3 cup olive oil

1/3 cup white wine vinegar

Juice of 2 lemons

4 tablespoons Italian herb seasoning

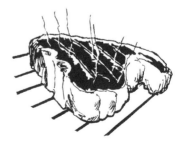 Combine all of the ingredients in a glass jar. Mix well and store in the refrigerator.

Makes about 1 cup

VERMOUTH MARINADE

A delicious marinade for smoking delicate fish like sole, trout, halibut, or orange roughy. It's also good on poultry.

1/2 cup dry vermouth

1/4 cup lemon juice

3 tablespoons butter

1 clove garlic, minced

1/2 teaspoon red pepper

In a small saucepan, combine all of the ingredients and simmer for several minutes. Store in a glass jar in the refrigerator for 2 to 3 weeks, or use immediately.

Makes 1 cup

Three Citrus Vinaigrette

*Fresh citrus makes seafood and poultry dance.
The lively tartness is wonderful for a summer
supper or fancy get-together! Variation: substitute different fruit juices to create your own
favorite combination—like pineapple, papaya,
or apricot juice.*

1/2 cup fresh orange juice

1/4 cup fresh lemon juice

1/4 cup fresh lime juice

1 tablespoon chopped fresh basil

1 tablespoon snipped fresh green onion
    or chives

2 tablespoons finely chopped red onion

1 cup olive oil

Salt and freshly ground pepper

Combine juices, basil, chives, and onion in a blender or food processor. While the motor is running, slowly add olive oil to emulsify. Season with salt and pepper and pour into a large glass jar or plastic container for storage in the refrigerator for 2 to 3 days. Use as a marinade, but it may also be drizzled over grilled meats and vegetables for a delicious dressing.

Makes 2 cups

Java Marinade

Use to marinate poultry, pork, or beef for the flavor of the exotic East.

1 cup strong coffee

1/2 cup cider vinegar

3/4 cup brown sugar

1/4 cup chopped onion

1 tablespoon oil

1 teaspoon dry mustard

Salt and pepper to taste

Combine all of the ingredients in a glass jar. Mix well and store in the refrigerator.

Makes about 2 cups

Minced Onion Marinade

Marinate a whole salmon in this concoction for about 1 hour, and then cook it in a smoker or on the grill.

1 small sweet white onion, minced

1/2 cup snipped fresh chives

1/3 cup freshly squeezed lemon juice

1/3 cup dry white wine

Salt and freshly ground black pepper to taste

Combine all of the ingredients in a glass jar. Shake to blend. Store in the refrigerator for up to 4 days.

Makes 1 cup

Spicy Horseradish Marinade

A versatile marinade or baste for beef, game, pork, or poultry.

1/3 cup olive oil

1/3 cup chili sauce

3 tablespoons horseradish

3 tablespoons lemon juice

3 tablespoons red wine

1/2 teaspoon dry mustard

1/2 teaspoon pepper

Combine all of the ingredients in a glass jar and mix well. Use immediately or store in the refrigerator for up to 7 days.

Makes 1 cup

Marmalade Marinade

This fresh, piquant marinade is perfect for pork and poultry.

1 lemon, quartered and seeded
1 large lime, quartered and seeded
$\frac{1}{2}$ cup sugar
1 tablespoon orange juice
1 tablespoon white vinegar

 Finely chop lemon and lime quarters in a food processor. Place chopped fruit in a glass bowl and stir in sugar, orange juice, and vinegar. Microwave on medium heat for 5 to 7 minutes, stirring several times. Store in a tightly covered container in the refrigerator for up to 21 days.

Makes about 1 cup

GINGER VINAIGRETTE

Marinate fish, pork, or poultry with this vinaigrette. Make extra to reserve as a salad dressing. It's delicious.

3 tablespoons chicken broth

3 tablespoons fresh lime juice

3 tablespoons fresh ginger, grated

2 tablespoons shallots, finely chopped

1 tablespoon honey

1 tablespoon soy sauce

1 clove garlic, minced

2 tablespoons olive oil

Combine all of the ingredients in a glass jar. Shake to blend. Store in the refrigerator for up to 4 days.

Makes 1 cup

Toasted Sesame-Soy Marinade and Dressing

Use half of this mixture as a marinade for salmon or chicken breasts for the grill. Serve meat over a bed of mixed greens and drizzle with the remaining mixture for a salad that's a complete meal.

1/2 cup olive oil

1/2 cup grapefruit juice

1/4 cup soy sauce

2 tablespoons toasted sesame oil

1 1/2 tablespoons sugar

2 teaspoons grated ginger

Combine all of the ingredients in a glass jar. Mix well and store in the refrigerator.

Makes about 1 1/2 cups

WHITE WINE VINAIGRETTE

Fresh vinaigrettes are easy to make, packed with flavor, and are the perfect all-purpose marinades.

1/2 cup olive oil

1/4 cup vinegar

1/4 cup dry white wine

1 clove garlic, minced

1/2 teaspoon mustard

1 teaspoon sugar

1/4 teaspoon salt

Pepper to taste

Combine all of the ingredients in a glass jar. Mix well and store in the refrigerator.

Makes about 3/4 cup

Spiked Italian Vinaigrette

Italian dressing is an ever-popular marinade. Here is just one way to improve on an already good thing!

1 cup Italian salad dressing

1/3 cup sweet red vermouth (or Italian red wine)

1 teaspoon dry mustard

1 teaspoon seasoned pepper

1 teaspoon celery seed

1 teaspoon minced roasted garlic

1 teaspoon sugar

1/2 teaspoon red pepper

 Combine all of the ingredients in a glass jar and shake to blend. Store in the refrigerator.

Makes about 1 1/3 cups

Apple Cider Marinade for Beef

For a variation, substitute chicken broth,
instead of beef broth, for marinating poultry.

1/2 cup apple cider (or apple juice)

1/2 cup beef broth

1/4 cup brown sugar

2 tablespoons cayenne pepper

2 teaspoons garlic powder

2 teaspoons celery salt

 Combine all of the ingredients in a glass jar. Mix well and store in the refrigerator.

Makes about 1 cup

Jammin' Cherry Marinade

Jams, jellies, and fruit preserves are flavorful bases for marinades. Because of the sugar content, use on meats that grill quickly, like boneless chicken breasts or thin pork chops, to avoid burning.

½ cup cherry preserves

2 tablespoons white wine vinegar

2 tablespoons sweet & hot mustard

1 jalapeño pepper, finely chopped

In a small saucepan, heat preserves to liquefy. Remove from heat and whisk in vinegar and mustard. Stir in jalapeño. Use immediately, or store in a glass jar in the refrigerator for 1 to 2 weeks. Gently heat to liquefy again before using.

Makes about ³/₄ cup

CRANBERRY VINAIGRETTE

This makes a thick vinaigrette that's perfect for marinating a pork roast, turkey breast, or whole chicken. Reserve 1/2 cup of vinaigrette and thin down with 2 tablespoons each oil and orange juice for a salad dressing.

1 cup cranberries

1/2 cup sugar

1/4 cup cider vinegar

1/4 cup orange juice

1/4 cup vegetable oil

1 teaspoon Dijon mustard

1/2 teaspoon red pepper flakes

1/2 teaspoon cinnamon

1/2 teaspoon garlic salt

In a large saucepan, heat the cranberries, sugar, and vinegar over medium heat until the cranberries pop, about 5 to 7 minutes. Remove from heat and add the remaining ingredients, whisking to blend well. Store in a glass container in the refrigerator for 1 to 2 weeks.

Makes about 2 1/2 cups

Tangy Teriyaki Marinade

Poultry, pork, and seafood take well to this marinade.

¹/₂ cup teriyaki

¹/₄ cup orange juice

3 tablespoons Chinese-style prepared mustard

¹/₄ teaspoon red pepper flakes

 Combine all of the ingredients in a glass jar and mix well. Store in the refrigerator for up to 2 weeks.

Makes about 1 cup

Blackberry Vinaigrette

Beef, venison, and elk meat combine well with this sweetly tangy berry vinaigrette.

1/2 cup blackberry jam

1/3 cup red wine vinegar

1/3 cup olive oil

2 cloves garlic, minced

1 teaspoon dry mustard

1/2 teaspoon cloves

1/2 teaspoon black pepper

1/4 teaspoon sea salt

In a small saucepan, gently heat jam to dissolve. Remove from heat and whisk with the remaining ingredients together in a bowl. Marinate meat of choice for several hours. Remove meat from marinade, put marinade in a saucepan, and bring to a boil to kill any bacteria from the uncooked meat. Serve the boiled marinade as a delicious finishing sauce.

Makes about 1 1/4 cups

Chimichurri Sauce

This traditional marinade from Argentina will wake up your grilled beef.

1 cup olive oil

1 cup sherry vinegar

½ cup chopped flat-leaf parsley

¼ cup chopped fresh oregano

¼ cup chopped onion

2 cloves garlic, minced

2 teaspoons cayenne pepper

1 teaspoon black pepper

½ teaspoon sea salt

Combine all of the ingredients in a glass jar and mix well. Store in the refrigerator for up to 2 weeks.

Makes about 3 cups

BIG HUNT MARINADE

This hearty marinade can handle a 2-pound venison loin.

1/2 cup olive oil

1/2 cup white wine

1/2 cup spicy mustard

1/4 cup minced shallots

2 tablespoons chopped fresh herbs (thyme, chives, savory, or oregano)

5 to 6 cloves garlic, chopped

Salt and freshly ground black pepper to taste

Combine all of the ingredients in a glass jar and mix well. Store in the refrigerator for up to 1 week.

Makes about 2 cups

Seasoning Salt

Use this mixture as a flavorful brine for the meat of your choice. It's also a wonderful gourmet gift from the kitchen.

1 cup sea salt

2 tablespoons paprika

1 teaspoon parsley flakes

1 teaspoon dried chives

1 teaspoon black pepper

1/2 teaspoon dried marjoram leaves

1/2 teaspoon celery seed

1/2 teaspoon curry powder

1/2 teaspoon garlic powder

1/4 teaspoon red pepper

Combine all of the ingredients in a glass jar. Shake to blend. Keeps for several months.

Makes 1 1/4 cups

Three Pepper Rub

This Southwest-style mixture is great on steaks, pork, and poultry. This recipe makes enough to coat 4 steaks.

2 tablespoons paprika

2 tablespoons seasoned black pepper

2 teaspoons white pepper

2 teaspoons ground red pepper

2 teaspoons brown sugar

1 teaspoon salt

1 teaspoon ground cumin

Combine all of the ingredients in a glass jar and cover with a tight-fitting lid. Store in a dark cupboard away from heat. Keeps for several weeks.

Makes about ¹/2 cup

Spicy Herb Rub

This is a delicious blend of spices for seafood, especially salmon.

1/2 cup parsley flakes

1/4 cup thyme

1/4 cup marjoram

1 tablespoon dried lemon peel

1 teaspoon red pepper flakes

1/2 teaspoon salt

Combine all of the ingredients in a glass jar and cover with a tight-fitting lid. Store in a dark cupboard away from heat. Keeps for several weeks.

Makes about 1 cup

Seasoned Bread Crumb Mix

Great for chicken breasts. Brush meat with some olive oil and then lightly coat with the bread crumb mixture. Grill or pan sauté in olive oil and serve hot or cold.

1/4 cup seasoned bread crumbs

1/4 cup seasoned black pepper

2 tablespoons oregano

2 teaspoons garlic powder

Salt to taste

Combine all of the ingredients in a glass jar and cover with a tight-fitting lid. Store in a dark cupboard away from heat. Keeps for several weeks.

Makes about 3/4 cup

Fresh Fines Herbes

Grill summer squash with olive oil, then toss with this fresh herb mix. Serve as a side dish or atop the pasta of your choice.

1/2 cup chopped fresh herbs (parsley, chives, tarragon)

Salt and freshly ground pepper to taste

Combine all of the ingredients in a glass bowl or jar. Use fresh herbs immediately.

Makes 1/2 cup

HOT CHICKEN WINGS SEASONING

This is a spicy blend, perfect for hot chicken wings. Dredge the wings in the spice mixture and let the wings sit for an hour. Wings may be grilled or smoked and served with a blue cheese dipping sauce.

1 1/2 cups barbecue spice

1 teaspoon ground red pepper

1 teaspoon black pepper or to taste

 Combine all of the ingredients in a glass jar and cover with a tight-fitting lid. Store in a dark cupboard away from heat. Keeps for several weeks.

Makes about 1 1/2 cups

Cumin-Coriander Rub

A simple blend of two aromatic spices, this is especially delicious on pork tenderloin.

1/4 cup cumin

1/4 cup coriander

 Combine the ingredients in a glass jar and cover with a tight-fitting lid. Store in a dark cupboard away from heat. Keeps for several weeks.

Makes 1/2 cup

Chile Pepper Rub

Control the heat in this rub by the kind of chiles you choose.

¹/₄ cup ground chiles

¹/₄ cup paprika

2 tablespoons black pepper

2 tablespoons salt

Combine all of the ingredients in a glass jar and cover with a tight-fitting lid. Store in a dark cupboard away from heat. Keeps for several weeks.

Makes ³/4 cup

Winter Sage Rub

Crumble this rub over a pork loin roast or turkey breast for a special holiday dinner.

1/4 cup dried basil leaves

2 tablespoons lemon pepper

1 tablespoon garlic powder

1 1/2 teaspoons sage

 Combine all of the ingredients in a glass jar and cover with a tight-fitting lid. Store in a dark cupboard away from heat. Keeps for several weeks.

Makes about 1/2 cup

ALL-PURPOSE RUB

As the name implies, you can rub into just about any kind of meat prior to cooking.

$1/2$ cup pepper

$1/2$ cup paprika

$1/4$ cup garlic powder

$1/4$ cup onion salt

$1/4$ cup dry mustard

$1/4$ cup celery seed

$1/4$ cup chili powder

$1/4$ cup brown sugar

1 tablespoon sea salt

Combine all of the ingredients in a glass jar and cover with a tight-fitting lid. Store in a dark cupboard away from heat. Keeps for several weeks.

Makes 2$1/2$ cups

Basic Brisket Rub

Simplicity is usually the rule for brisket rubs. When applying this rub, first coat the brisket with olive oil and then sprinkle liberally with the dry rub.

1/2 cup paprika

1/4 cup cayenne pepper

1/4 cup granulated garlic

1/4 cup black pepper

Combine all of the ingredients in a glass jar and cover with a tight-fitting lid. Store in a dark cupboard away from heat. Keeps for several weeks.

Makes 1 1/4 cups

Brisket Rub Texas-Style

*Patience is the key to slow-smoking brisket. Apply the rub
to the meat and marinate overnight in the refrigerator.
Cook the brisket over 225- to 250-degree heat very slowly
for about 1 hour per pound of meat.*

3/4 cup coarse salt

1/4 cup black pepper

1/4 cup lemon pepper

2 tablespoons dried chipotle chiles (or chili powder)

2 tablespoons dried thyme

2 tablespoons paprika

2 tablespoons cumin

2 tablespoons garlic powder

2 tablespoons cayenne pepper

Combine all of the ingredients in a glass jar and
cover with a tight-fitting lid. Store in a dark cupboard
away from heat. Keeps for several weeks.

Makes 2 cups

Memphis Rib Rub

*This makes enough to sprinkle over 2 slabs of ribs.
Cook in a smoker at 225 degrees F for about
4 hours. Coat ribs with a thin glaze of honey for
the last 30 minutes of cooking.*

3 tablespoons paprika

1½ tablespoons dry mustard

1 tablespoon onion powder

1 tablespoon garlic powder

1 tablespoon ground basil

1 tablespoon red pepper

½ tablespoon black pepper

Combine all of the ingredients and rub onto
ribs. Or place in a glass jar and cover with a tight-
fitting lid. Store in a dark cupboard away from
heat. Keeps for several weeks.

Makes about ½ cup

Aromatic Herb Rub for Duck

This makes enough rub to season 8 whole ducklings for the oven or the smoker.

^{1}/2 cup paprika

^{1}/3 cup lemon pepper

^{1}/3 cup black pepper

^{1}/3 cup white pepper

^{1}/4 cup garlic salt

^{1}/4 cup brown sugar, packed

2 tablespoons dried rosemary

2 tablespoons fennel

2 tablespoons anise

Combine all of the ingredients in a glass jar and cover with a tight-fitting lid. Store in a dark cupboard away from heat. Keeps for several weeks.

Makes 2^1/3 cups

Ginger Spiced Rub for Pork

*Generously coat a pork roast or Boston butt
with this pungent spice blend. Wrap in plastic
and refrigerate for 3 to 4 hours or overnight.
A nice apricot and teriyaki basting sauce is a fine
complement to this rub.*

1/4 cup brown sugar, packed

2 tablespoon lemon pepper

1 tablespoon ground ginger

1 tablespoon onion salt

1 tablespoon chili powder

1 tablespoon dried oregano

1 teaspoon dried thyme

1 teaspoon garlic powder

1/2 teaspoon ground cloves

Combine all of the ingredients in a glass jar
and cover with a tight-fitting lid. Store in a dark
cupboard away from heat. Keeps for several weeks.

Makes 1/2 cup

Que Queens' Prize-Winning Rib Rub

The celery salt adds a dimension to this rub that marries perfectly with pork, especially ribs.

2 tablespoons brown sugar

2 tablespoons pepper

2 tablespoons paprika

1 tablespoon celery salt

1 tablespoon garlic salt

 Combine all of the ingredients in a glass jar and cover with a tight-fitting lid. Store in a dark cupboard away from heat. Keeps for several weeks.

Makes 1/2 cup

Que Queens' Royal Rub

Lou Jane Temple shares this from her culinary murder mystery Revenge of the Barbecue Queens.

¼ cup mixed peppercorns (black, white, and pink)

¼ cup mustard seeds

¼ cup sesame seeds, lightly toasted

¼ cup kosher salt

1 dried ancho chile

¼ cup New Mexican ground red chili

¼ cup brown sugar

¼ cup hot Hungarian paprika

1 tablespoon each cinnamon, cumin, rubbed sage, cayenne, allspice, dried thyme, and dried tarragon

Preheat oven to 350 degrees F. Combine the peppercorns, mustard seeds, sesame seeds, salt, and ancho chile in the food processor and pulverize. Combine this mixture with the remaining ingredients, taking care to mix carefully as it will cause sneezing. Spread on baking sheets and toast in oven for 10 minutes, checking occasionally to make sure mixture doesn't burn.

Store in a glass jar covered with a tight-fitting lid in a dark cupboard away from heat. Keeps for several weeks.

Makes about 2 cups

Cinnamon Spice Rub

The cinnamon and allspice give a holiday aroma to this all-purpose rub.

1 tablespoon chili powder

1 tablespoon curry powder

1 tablespoon paprika

$1/2$ tablespoon allspice

$1/2$ tablespoon cinnamon

$1/2$ tablespoon mace

$1/2$ tablespoon pepper

Combine all of the ingredients in a glass jar and cover with a tight-fitting lid. Store in a dark cupboard away from heat. Keeps for several weeks.

Makes about $1/4$ cup

Herb Rub for Lamb

Always crumble or rub herbs between the palms of your hands to release the herbs' oils and to maximize flavor.

2 tablespoons each dried basil, oregano, parsley, and savory

2 teaspoons each dried thyme, sage, and rosemary

1 teaspoon dried fennel

Combine all of the ingredients in a glass jar and cover with a tight-fitting lid. Store in a dark cupboard away from heat. Keeps for several weeks.

Makes 2/3 cup

Parsley, Sage, Rosemary, and Thyme

Just like the song, this herb combination is a winner.

1 cup assorted dry herbs (parsley, sage, rosemary, and thyme)

1 tablespoon freshly ground pepper

 Combine all of the ingredients in a glass jar and cover with a tight-fitting lid. Store in a dark cupboard away from heat. Keeps for several weeks.

Makes about 1 cup

Lemon-Lime Rub

A delightful, zesty marinade that is perfect for pork, poultry, and seafood. It's lovely sprinkled on summer or winter squash that you cook on the grill.

¼ cup dried lemon zest

¼ cup dried lime zest

½ cup brown sugar

1 tablespoon seasoned pepper

Combine all of the ingredients in a glass jar and cover with a tight-fitting lid. Store in a dark cupboard away from heat. Keeps for several weeks.

Makes 1 cup

Red Pepper-Herb Rub

This is a zesty herb rub that has some kick.
Great for poultry and seafood.

1/4 cup dried lemon peel

1/4 cup dried basil

1/4 cup dried tarragon

1 tablespoon garlic powder

1/2 tablespoon white pepper

1 teaspoon sea salt

1 teaspoon red pepper flakes

Combine all of the ingredients in a glass jar and cover with a tight-fitting lid. Store in a dark cupboard away from heat. Keeps for several weeks.

Makes about 1 cup

Jerk Rub

For best results, sprinkle this rub over pork, poultry, or fish. It makes enough to marinate 2 pounds of meat.

2 tablespoons allspice

2 tablespoons cinnamon

2 tablespoons paprika

2 tablespoons dried thyme

2 tablespoons brown sugar

2 teaspoons freshly grated nutmeg

2 teaspoons powdered ginger

2 teaspoons red pepper

1 teaspoon black pepper

1 teaspoon white pepper

1 teaspoon salt

Combine all of the ingredients in a glass jar and cover with a tight-fitting lid. Store in a dark cupboard away from heat. Keeps for several weeks.

Makes about 1 cup

SPICE RUB

*Try this fragrant mixture on a whole chicken
and serve with sautéed sweet potato slices dusted
lightly with the same rub.*

¼ cup garlic powder

¼ cup onion powder

2 tablespoons allspice

2 tablespoons brown sugar

1 tablespoon dried ground chipotle chile

1 tablespoon dried thyme

1 tablespoon cinnamon

2 teaspoons dried lemon zest

1 teaspoon cloves

1 teaspoon nutmeg

½ teaspoon ground habanero chili powder

Combine all of the ingredients in a glass jar
and cover with a tight-fitting lid. Store in a dark
cupboard away from heat. Keeps for several weeks.

Makes about 1 cup

Herbes de Provence

This is a good blend for meat, fish, and vegetables. Customize it by adding your own favorite dried herbs.

3 tablespoons dried thyme

3 tablespoons dried rosemary

3 bay leaves

2 tablespoons dried basil

2 tablespoons dried marjoram

1 1/2 teaspoons fennel seeds

1 teaspoon summer savory

1 teaspoon dried lavender flowers

Combine all of the ingredients, leaving the bay leaves whole. Make the blend ahead of time for the bay leaves to infuse the mixture. Discard the bay leaves when using the blend. Store in a dark cupboard in a glass jar with a tight-fitting lid.

Makes about 1/3 cup

Blackened Seasoning

A blackened seasoning gets best results when grilled quickly over very high heat. This sears the meat and blackens the seasoning for a dark, pungent crust.

1/4 cup lemon pepper

1/4 cup paprika

1 tablespoon sea salt

1 tablespoon white pepper

1 tablespoon garlic powder

1 teaspoon cumin

1 teaspoon ground red pepper

Combine all of the ingredients in a glass jar and cover with a tight-fitting lid. Store in a dark cupboard away from heat. Keeps for several weeks.

Makes about 3/4 cup

CREOLE MUSTARD PASTE

An excellent spicy paste for catfish, swordfish, or any whitefish.

1/2 cup Creole mustard

1/4 cup blackened seasoning (page 84)

1 medium onion, finely chopped

3 cloves garlic, minced

1 tablespoon hot sauce

 Combine all of the ingredients in a glass jar and cover with a tight-fitting lid. Store in the refrigerator. Keeps for several weeks.

Makes about 1 cup

Italian Parmesan Paste

This is a lovely thick paste that is great for marinating boneless chicken breasts, pork chops or tenderloin, and even a nice thick beef tenderloin or fillet. Marinate for only 1 to 2 hours.

1/2 cup grated Parmesan cheese

1/4 cup olive oil

1/4 cup red wine vinegar

2 tablespoons dried basil

2 tablespoons dried oregano

1 tablespoon seasoned pepper

4 cloves garlic, minced

Combine all of the ingredients and apply to poultry, beef, or pork. Or store in a glass jar for 2 to 3 days before using.

Makes about 1 1/2 cups

Moroccan Spice Paste

This aromatic marinade works well with poultry, lamb, and seafood. Marinate poultry and lamb overnight in the refrigerator. Marinate seafood for only 30 to 60 minutes.

1 small onion, chopped

½ cup olive oil

2 tablespoons lemon juice

½ cup chopped fresh cilantro

½ cup chopped fresh flat-leaf parsley

4 cloves garlic, minced

1 tablespoon paprika

2 teaspoons ginger

2 teaspoons sea salt

1 teaspoon cumin

½ teaspoon turmeric

Combine all of the ingredients in a food processor and blend. Use immediately or store in a glass container in the refrigerator for 1 to 2 days.

Makes about 2 cups

Caesar Salad Paste

This is a lovely, pungent paste that is excellent on tuna, swordfish, and chicken breast.

4 to 6 anchovy fillets

1 tablespoon capers, optional

3/4 cup olive oil

1/2 cup grated Romano cheese

1/3 cup lemon juice

In a small bowl, mash the anchovies and capers together. Add the remaining ingredients and whisk to blend. Store in a glass container in the refrigerator for up to 1 week.

Makes about 1 1/2 cups

Fresh Garlic-Parsley Paste

These ingredients create a simple pesto-style paste that almost any palate will like.

1/2 cup fresh parsley

6 cloves garlic, minced

1 teaspoon cayenne pepper

Juice and zest of 1 lemon

1/3 cup olive oil

In a food processor, add parsley, garlic, cayenne pepper, lemon juice and zest. Slowly add oil in a thin stream while continuing to mix. Store in an air-tight container in the refrigerator for up to 5 days.

Makes about 1/2 cup

Rosemary-Dijon Paste

This is a savory marinade that enhances pork, poultry, and seafood. Use a pastry brush to coat meat or vegetables prior to grilling.

1 cup Dijon mustard

1/2 cup chopped fresh parsley

1/2 cup chopped fresh rosemary

2 tablespoons white wine Worcestershire sauce

2 tablespoons seasoned black pepper

Juice and zest of 1 lemon

Sea salt to taste

Combine all of the ingredients. Store in an airtight container in the refrigerator for up to 5 days.

Makes 1 cup

Vidalia Onion Paste

This is an all-around blend that's good on meat and vegetables alike.

1 large Vidalia onion, quartered

1/4 cup white wine vinegar

1/4 cup olive oil

4 cloves of garlic

2 tablespoons dry mustard

2 tablespoons brown sugar

1 teaspoon red pepper flakes

In a food processor, combine all of the ingredients and process to a paste. Store in an airtight container in the refrigerator for 2 to 3 days.

Makes about 2 cups

Spinach Paste

Try pounding some turkey breast very thin and then spreading the spinach mixture over the meat. Roll the meat and secure with twine. Voilà! A rolled roast that can be smoked for a gourmet meal. After smoking, let the roast rest for about 20 to 30 minutes. Slice and serve.

1 pound fresh spinach, chopped

3 tablespoons chopped parsley

1/4 cup snipped dried apple

1/4 cup chopped dates

4 strips of bacon

1/4 cup chopped onion

2 cloves garlic, minced

1/2 cup chopped green onions

1/2 teaspoon each chopped fresh basil, marjoram, and rosemary

Salt and pepper to taste

In a large pan, bring 2 cups water to a boil. Add the chopped spinach and blanch by cooking for 2 minutes, then drain. (May use chopped frozen spinach, thawed and drained well.) In a large bowl, combine spinach with parsley, apple, and dates. In a sauté pan, cook bacon until crisp, set aside to cool, then crumble into spinach mixture. In the bacon drippings, sauté onion and garlic until tender, about 5 minutes. Add onion, herbs, salt, and pepper to spinach mixture and refrigerate to chill.

Spinach paste can be spread thinly over the meat of your choice before grilling. Or use the mixture for any rolled roast; it is especially delicious with leg of lamb.

Makes about 2 1/2 cups

Wasabi Grilling Paste

Wasabi is Japanese horseradish. It is available in paste form or as a dry powder. This yogurt or mayonnaise mixture is tasty as a marinade for poultry or seafood. Try mixing it with grilled or smoked potatoes for a tangy potato salad.

1 cup plain yogurt or mayonnaise

1 tablespoon wasabi paste

1/2 teaspoon dry mustard

Salt and pepper to taste

Combine all of the ingredients and use immediately.

Makes about 1 cup

BOOKS ON BARBECUE

The popularity of cookbooks available for grill and barbecue enthusiasts is ever growing. Here is a list of favorites, some old and some new. For a complete list of titles on outdoor cooking, visit www.pigoutpublications.com.

Barbecue America by Rick Browne & Jack Bettridge
    (1999, Time Life Books)
Barbecue Bible by Steven Raichlen (1998, Workman Publishing)
Barbecue Inferno by Dave DeWitt (2000, Ten Speed Press)
Barbecuing & Sausage Making Secrets by Charlie and Ruthie Knote
    (1993, Culinary Institute of Smoke Cooking)
Great BBQ Sauce Book by Ardie Davis (1999, Ten Speed Press)
Great Ribs Book by Hugh Carpenter and Teri Sandison
    (1999, Ten Speed Press)
Hooked on Fish on the Grill by Karen Adler (1992, Pig Out Publications)
Hot Barbecue! by Hugh Carpenter and Teri Sandison
    (1996, Ten Speed Press)
Grilling Encyclopedia by A. Cort Sinnes (1992, Atlantic Monthly Press)
Indian Grill by Smita Chandra (1999, Harper Collins)
Passion of Barbeque by the Kansas City Barbeque Society
    (1992, Hyperion)
Que Queens–Easy Grilling & Simple Smoking by Karen Adler &
    Judith Fertig (1997, Pig Out Publications)
Smoke & Spice by Cheryl and Bill Jamison
    (1995, Harvard Common Press)
Wild about Kansas City Barbecue by Rich Davis and Shifra Stein
    (2000, Pig Out Publications)

CONVERSIONS

LIQUID
1 tablespoon = 15 milliliters
1/2 cup = 4 fluid ounces = 125 milliliters
1 cup = 8 fluid ounces = 250 milliliters

DRY
1/4 cup = 4 tablespoons = 2 ounces = 60 grams
1 cup = 1/2 pound = 8 ounces = 250 grams

FLOUR
1/2 cup = 60 grams
1 cup = 4 ounces = 125 grams

TEMPERATURE
400 degrees F = 200 degrees C = gas mark 6
375 degrees F = 190 degrees C = gas mark 5
350 degrees F = 175 degrees C = gas mark 4

MISCELLANEOUS
2 tablespoons butter = 1 ounce = 30 grams
1 inch = 2.5 centimeters
all purpose flour = plain flour
baking soda = bicarbonate of soda
brown sugar= demerara sugar
confectioners' sugar = icing sugar
heavy cream = double cream
molasses= black treacle
raisins = sultanas
rolled oats = oat flakes
semisweet chocolate = plain chocolate
sugar= caster sugar